Now you can be the feature trumpet soloist on eight specially recorded arrangements

jazz

TAKE THE LEAD

trumpet

IMP

International MUSIC Publications

International Music Publications Limited
Griffin House 161 Hammersmith Road London W6 8BS England

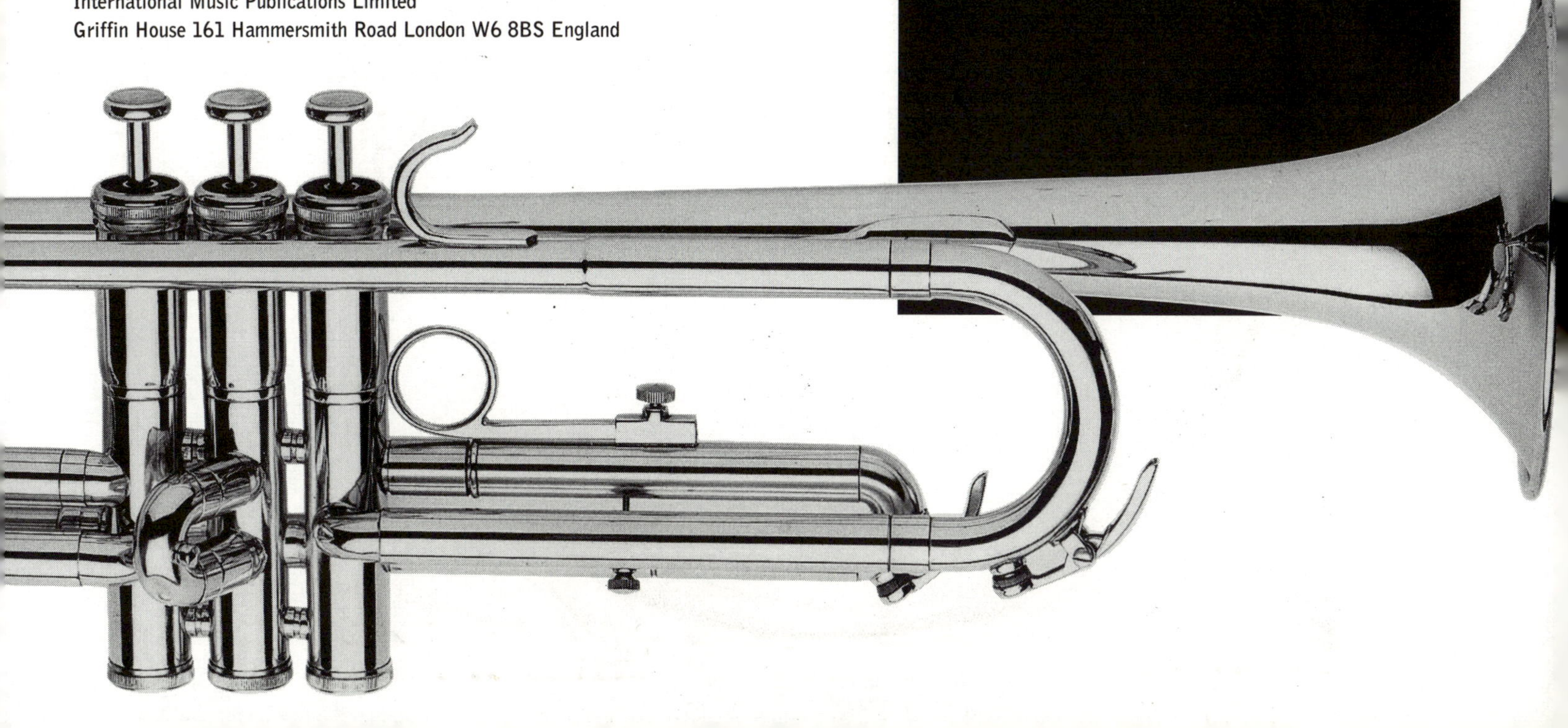

Series Editor: Sadie Cook

Editorial, production and recording: Artemis Music Limited
Design and production: Space DPS Limited

Published 1999

IMP
International
MUSIC
Publications

IMP
International Music Publications Limited

England: Griffin House
161 Hammersmith Road
London W6 8BS

Germany: Marstallstr. 8
D-80539 München

Denmark: Danmusik
Vognmagergade 7
DK1120 Copenhagen K

Carisch

Italy: Via Campania 12
20098 San Giuliano Milanese
Milano

Spain: Magallanes 25
28015 Madrid

France: 20 Rue de la Ville-l'Eveque
75008 Paris

trumpet

TAKE THE LEAD

In the Book...

On the CD...

Track **1** Tuning Tones (A Concert)

Birdland

Track **2** Full version

Track **3** Backing track

Desafinado

Track **4** Full version

Track **5** Backing track

Don't Get Around Much Anymore

Track **6** Full version

Track **7** Backing track

Fascinating Rhythm

Track **8** Full version

Track **9** Backing track

Misty

Track **10** Full version

Track **11** Backing track

My Funny Valentine

Track **12** Full version

Track **13** Backing track

One O'Clock Jump

Track **14** Full version

Track **15** Backing track

Summertime

Track **16** Full version

Track **17** Backing track

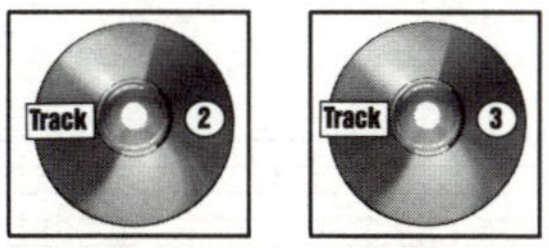

Demonstration Backing

Birdland

Music by
Josef Zawinul

43
47
G
mf
51
Bm7(b5)
57
9
f
G Bm Em G/B Cmaj C#dim Bm7 E7
70
(78)
Am C/G G Bm Em C6 C#m7(b5) C/D Cmaj9 Am9 C/D G
83
G/F# Em G/D C#m7(b5) Cmaj7 Bm7 E7 Am C/D G
87
G/F# Em G/D C#m7(b5) Cmaj7 Bm7 E7 Am C/D
91
G
mf
97
101
Gm F/G F/Bb Eb/Bb Dm7
ff

105
F/C E♭/C F/B G6 Gm/C F/E♭
109
G Gm/C F/C
mp
113
117
G Bm Em G/B Cmaj C♯dim Bm7
f
121
(129)
E7 Am C/G G Bm Em C6 C♯m7(♭5) C/D Cmaj9
125
(133)
Am9 C/D G G/F♯ Em G/D C♯m7(♭5) Cmaj7 Bm7
137
E7 Am C/D G G/F♯ Em G/D C♯m7(♭5) Cmaj7 Bm7 E7
142
Am C/D G/F♯ Em G/D C♯m7(♭5) Cmaj7 Bm7 E7 Am C/D G
147
G/F♯ Em G/D C♯m7(♭5) Cmaj7 Bm7 E7 Am C/D G

Demonstration Backing

Desafinado

Words by Newton Ferriera de Mendonca
Music by Antonio Carlos Jobim

45 Amaj7 F#m7 Bm7 E7 Cmaj7
50 C#dim7 Dm7 G7 Gm7 Ebm6
55 G7 C7 Fmaj7 G7(b5)
60 (80) Gm7 C7 Am7(b5) D7
65 (85) Gm7 Bbm6 Fmaj7 Am7/D G7
70 (90) Eb9 1. G7 Gm7 C7
75 F 2. G7 Gm7 C7 F
96 D7 G7 Gm7 C7 F
rall.
100 D7 G7 Gm7 C7 F

Don't Get Around Much Anymore

Demonstration Backing

Music by Duke Ellington

55 C F6 F♯dim G F♯dim
61 C A7 4 N.C. C
f
70 A7 N.C. D7 G7
75 C N.C. C A7
81 D7 G7 C F6
86 Fm C F6 F♯dim G F♯dim
92 G N.C. C A7
97 D7 G7 Em7 A7
101 D7 G C
p

Fascinating Rhythm

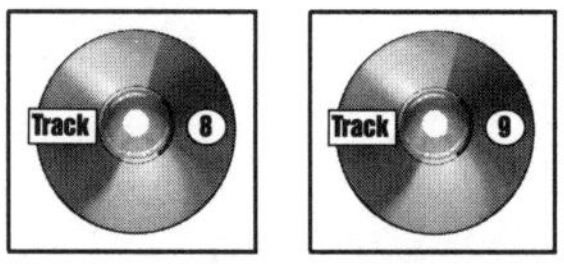

Demonstration Backing

Music and Lyrics by
George Gershwin and Ira Gershwin

42 C7 Gm7 C7 Gm7 C7 Gm7 C7 Gm7 C F Bm7(b5) E7
47 Am D7 G7 Dm7 G7 Dm7 G7 D7 G13 C6
53 G7 Dm7 G7 Dm7 G7 Dm7 G7 Dm7 G7 Dm7 G7 Dm7 G7
p
57 C7 Gm7 C7 Gm7 C7 Gm7 C7 Gm7 C7 Gm7 C7 Gm7 C7
61 F Am7 Dm7 G7 C Am Am7 D7 D13
mf
67 G7 A7 G7 Dm7 G7 Dm7 G7 Dm7 G7 Dm7 G7 Dm7 G7 Dm7
p
72 G7 C7 Gm7 C7 Gm7 C7 Gm7 C7 Gm7 C7 Gm7 C7 Gm7
76 C F Bm7(b5) E7 Am D7
f
81 G7 Dm7 G7 Dm7 G7 D7 G13 C6

Misty

Demonstration

Backing

Music by Erroll Garner

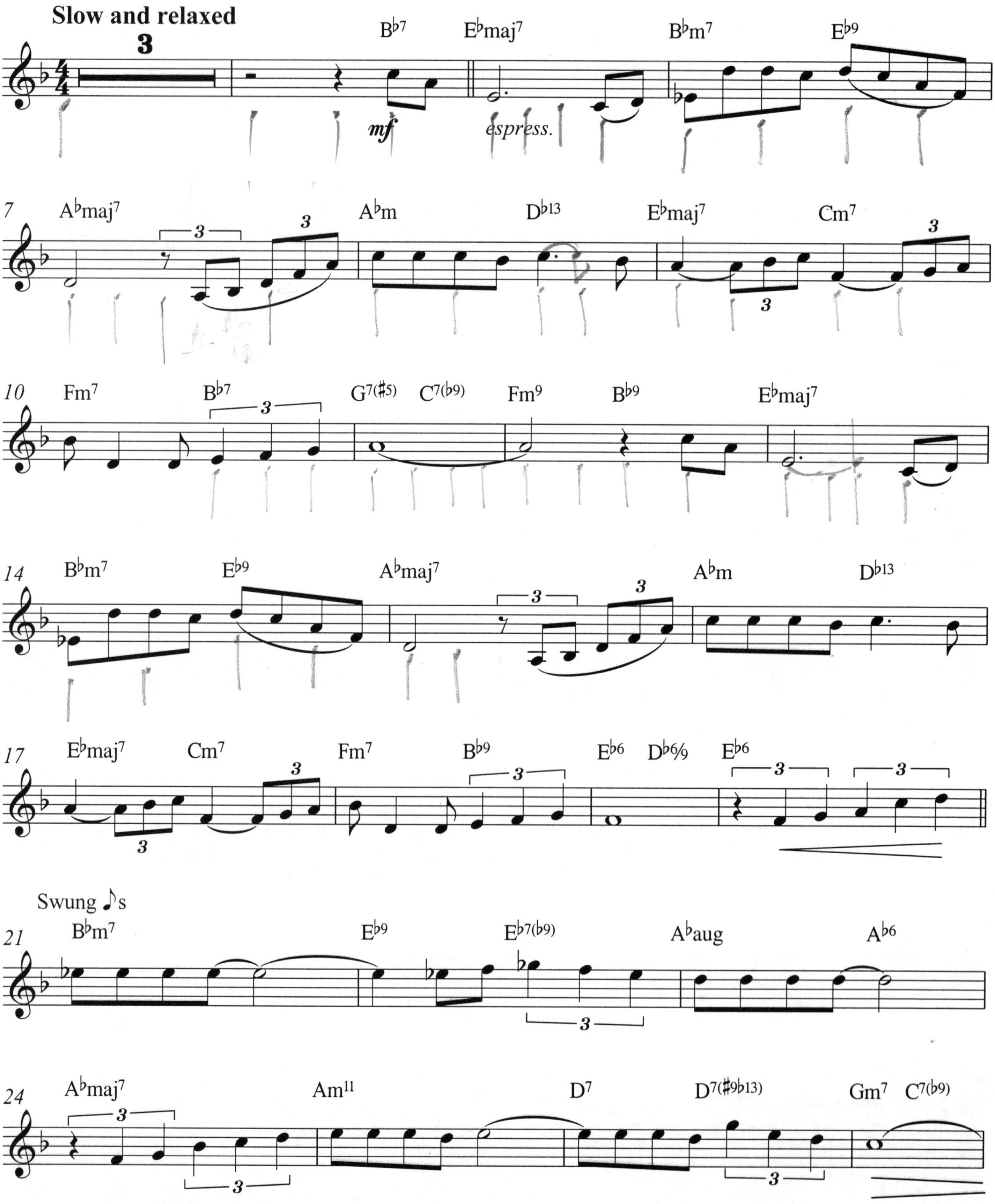

28 Fm11 B♭7(♭9) Straight ♪s E♭maj7 B♭m7 E♭9
31 A♭maj7 A♭m D♭13 E♭maj7 Cm7
34 Fm7 B♭9 E♭6 D♭6/9 E♭6 Swung ♪s B♭m7
38 E♭9 E♭7(♭9) A♭aug A♭6 A♭maj7 Am11
42 D7 D7(♯9♭13) Gm7 C7(♭9) Fm11 B♭7(♭9) Straight ♪s E♭maj7
46 B♭m7 E♭9 A♭maj7 A♭m D♭13
49 E♭maj7 Cm7 Fm7 B♭9 E♭maj7 Cm7 Fm7 B♭9
53 G7(♯5) Cm7 Fm7 B♭7(♭9) E♭6
mp

Demonstration

Backing

My Funny Valentine

Music by Richard Rodgers

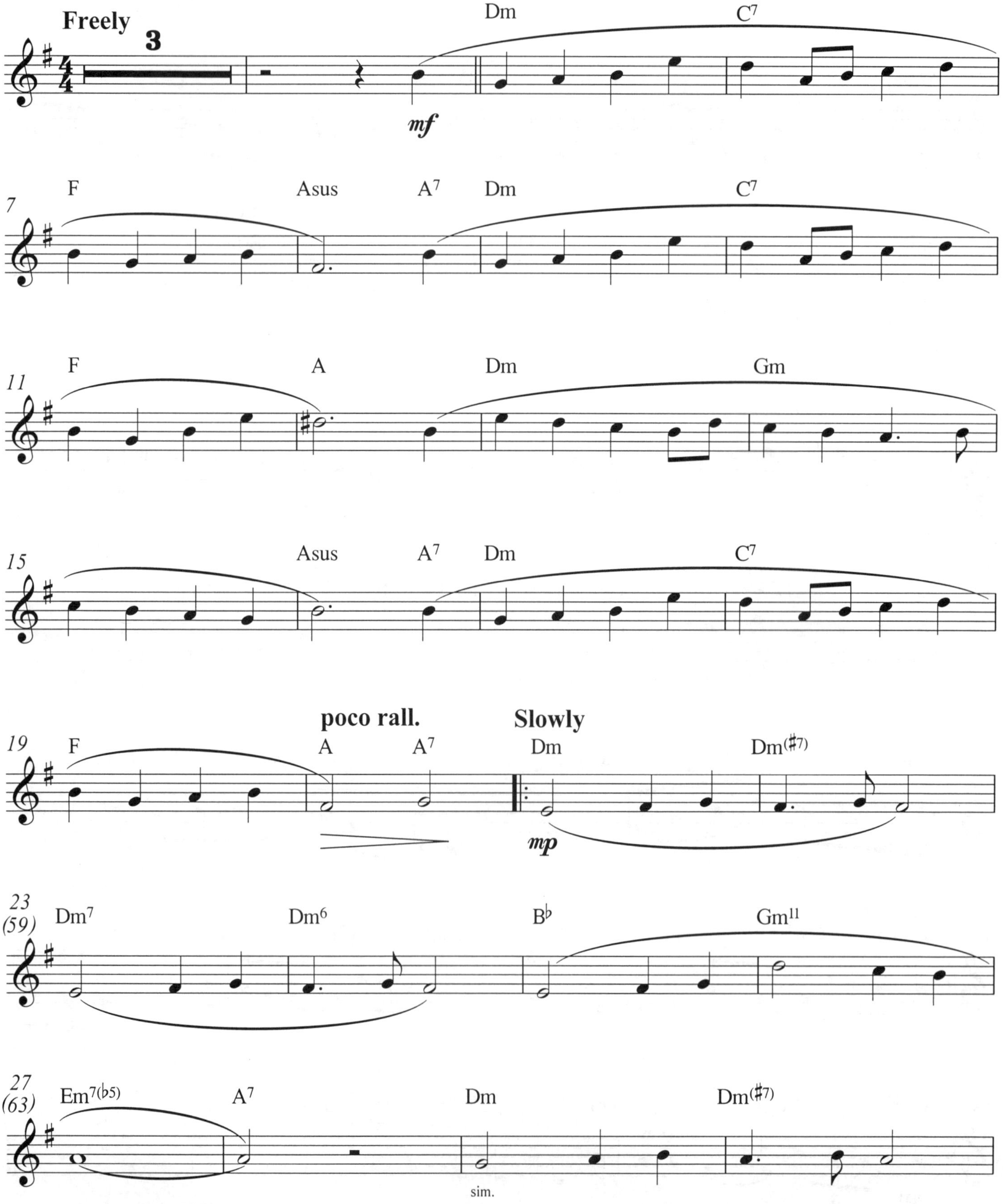

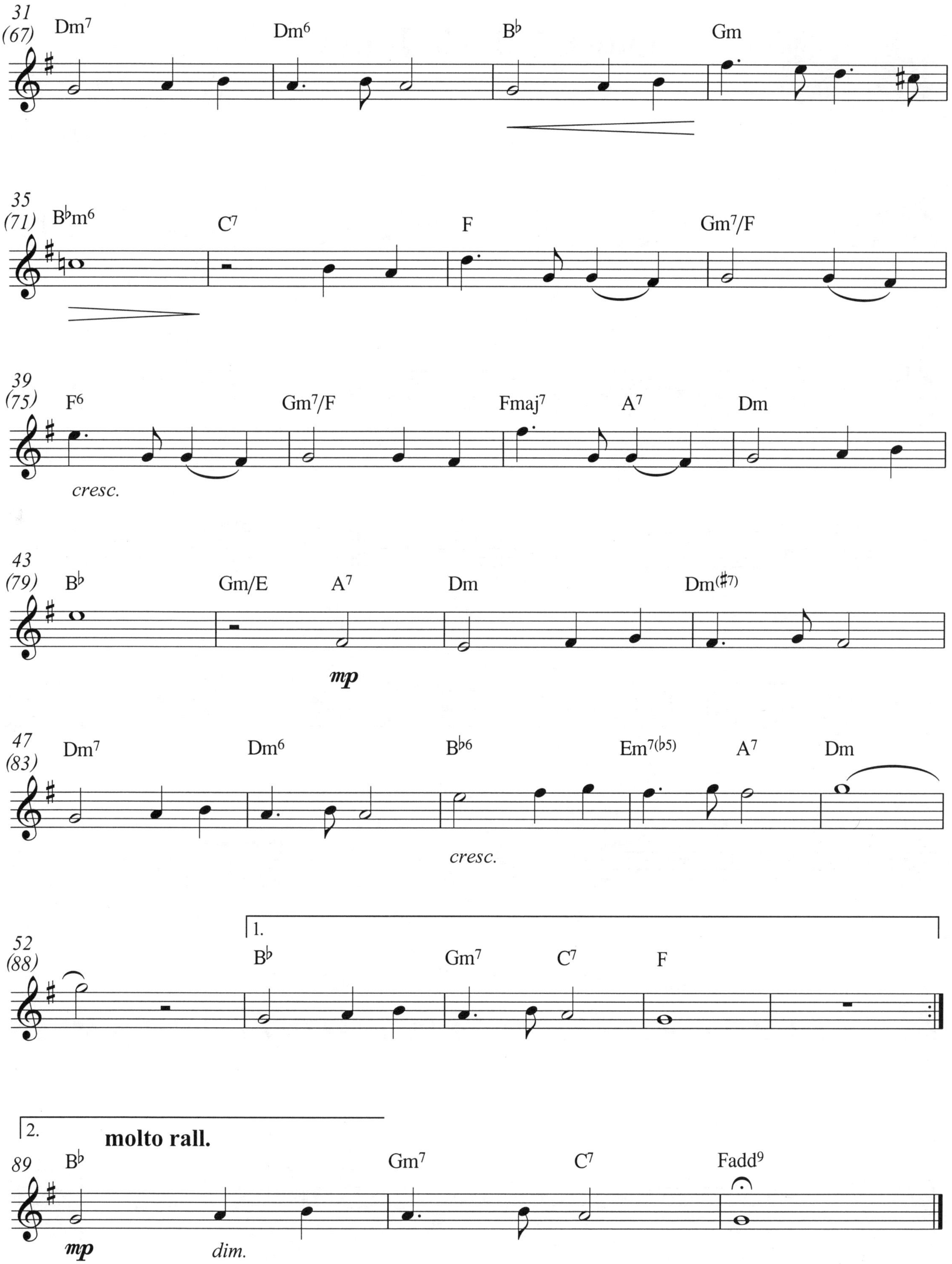
31
(67)
Dm7
Dm6
B♭
Gm
35
(71)
B♭m6
C7
F
Gm7/F
39
(75)
F6
Gm7/F
Fmaj7
A7
Dm
cresc.
43
(79)
B♭
Gm/E
A7
Dm
Dm(♯7)
mp
47
(83)
Dm7
Dm6
B♭6
Em7(♭5)
A7
Dm
cresc.
1.
52
(88)
B♭
Gm7
C7
F
2.
molto rall.
89
B♭
Gm7
C7
Fadd9
mp
dim.

One O'Clock Jump

Demonstration

Backing

Music by Count Basie

73
(85)
C7
f
77
(89)
F7
C7
81
(93)
G7
F7
C7
97
C7
f
F7
C7
F7
102
C7
Dm7
G7
107
C7
C7
mp
F7
C7
112
F7
C7
117
Dm7
cresc.
G7
C
Straight ♪s
f

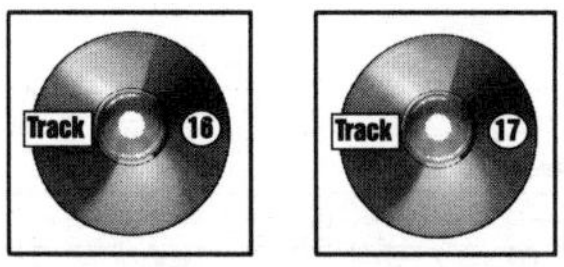

Demonstration Backing

Summertime

Music and Lyrics by George Gershwin,
Du Bose and Dorothy Heyward and Ira Gershwin

Reproduced and printed by
Halstan & Co. Ltd., Amersham, Bucks., England

3/00

You can be the featured soloist with TAKE THE LEAD

Collect these titles, each with demonstration and full backing tracks on CD.

90s Hits

The Air That I Breathe
(Simply Red)

Angels
(Robbie Williams)

How Do I Live
(LeAnn Rimes)

I Don't Want To Miss A Thing
(Aerosmith)

I'll Be There For You
(The Rembrandts)

My Heart Will Go On
(Celine Dion)

Something About The Way You Look Tonight
(Elton John)

Frozen
(Madonna)

Order ref: 6725A – Flute
Order ref: 6726A – Clarinet
Order ref: 6727A – Alto Saxophone
Order ref: 6728A – Violin

Movie Hits

Because You Loved Me
(Up Close And Personal)

Blue Monday
(The Wedding Singer)

(Everything I Do) I Do It For You
(Robin Hood: Prince Of Thieves)

I Don't Want To Miss A Thing
(Armageddon)

I Will Always Love You
(The Bodyguard)

Star Wars (Main Title)
(Star Wars)

The Wind Beneath My Wings
(Beaches)

You Can Leave Your Hat On
(The Full Monty)

Order ref: 6908A – Flute
Order ref: 6909A – Clarinet
Order ref: 6910A – Alto Saxophone
Order ref: 6911A –Tenor Saxophone
Order ref: 6912A – Violin

TV Themes

Coronation Street

I'll Be There For You (theme from *Friends*)

Match Of The Day

(Meet) The Flintstones

Men Behaving Badly

Peak Practice

The Simpsons

The X-Files

Order ref: 7003A – Flute
Order ref: 7004A – Clarinet
Order ref: 7005A – Alto Saxophone
Order ref: 7006A – Violin

Christmas Songs

The Christmas Song (Chestnuts Roasting On An Open Fire)

Frosty The Snowman

Have Yourself A Merry Little Christmas

Little Donkey

Rudolph The Red-Nosed Reindeer

Santa Claus Is Comin' To Town

Sleigh Ride

Winter Wonderland

Order ref: 7022A – Flute
Order ref: 7023A – Clarinet
Order ref: 7024A – Alto Saxophone
Order ref: 7025A – Violin
Order ref: 7026A – Piano
Order ref: 7027A – Drums

The Blues Brothers

She Caught The Katy And Left Me A Mule To Ride

Gimme Some Lovin'

Shake A Tail Feather

Everybody Needs Somebody To Love

The Old Landmark

Think

Minnie The Moocher

Sweet Home Chicago

Order ref: 7079A - Flute
Order ref: 7080A - Clarinet
Order ref: 7081A - Alto Saxophone
Order ref: 7082A - Tenor Saxophone
Order ref: 7083A - Trumpet
Order ref: 7084A - Violin